# DESTINATION: SPACE

SEYMOUR SIMON

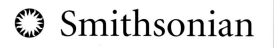
Smithsonian

Collins
*An Imprint of HarperCollinsPublishers*

To Jeremy, Chloe, Benjamin, and Joel

Happy exploring!

PHOTO CREDITS:
p. 4, C. Fritz Benedict, Andrew Howell, Inger Jorgensen, David Chapell (University of Texas), Jeffery Kenney (Yale University),
Beverly J. Smith (Columbia Aeronautic and Space Association, University of Colorado), NASA; inset, p. 4, NASA; p. 7, Philip James
(University of Toledo), Steven Lee (University of Colorado), NASA; p. 8, J.T. Trauger (Jet Propulsion Laboratory), NASA; p. 11, NASA,
Ron Gililand (Space Telescope Science Institute); p. 12, NASA, P. Challis, R. Kirshner (Harvard-Smithsonian Center for Astrophysics)
and B. Sugarman; p.14, Hubble Heritage Team, Association of Universities for Research in Astronomy/STScI/NASA; p. 17, Jeff Hester
and Paul Scowen (Arizona State University), NASA; p. 19, Wolfgang Bradner (JPL/IPAC), Eva K. Grebel (University of Washington),
You-Hua Chu (University of Illinois, Urbana-Champaign), NASA; p. 20, C. Robert O'Dell, Kerry P. Handron (Rice University), NASA;
p. 23, Bruce Balick (University of Washington), Vincent Icke (Leiden University, The Netherlands), Garrelt Mellema (Stockholm
University), NASA; p. 25, Brad Whitmore, STScI, NASA; p. 27, NASA, Hubble Heritage (STScI/AURA); p. 28, Marijn Franx (University of
Groningen, The Netherlands), Garth Illingworth (University of California, Santa Cruz), NASA; p. 31, L. Ferrarese (JHU) and NASA;
p. 32, R. Williams (STScI), the Hubble Deep Field South Team, NASA
The name of the Smithsonian, Smithsonian Institution and the sunburst logo
are registered trademarks of the Smithsonian Institution.
Collins is an imprint of HarperCollins Publishers.

Destination: Space
Copyright © 2002 by Seymour Simon
Introduction copyright © 2006 Smithsonian Institution
Manufactured in China. All rights reserved.
No part of this book may be used or reproduced in any manner whatsoever without written permission except in the case of brief
quotations embodied in critical articles and reviews. For information address HarperCollins Children's Books, a division of
HarperCollins Publishers, 1350 Avenue of the Americas, New York, NY 10019.
www.harperchildrens.com
Library of Congress Cataloging-in-Publication Data
Simon, Seymour.
Destination: space / Seymour Simon.
p.   cm.
Summary: Explains new discoveries about the universe made possible by the Hubble Telescope.
ISBN-10: 0-06-087722-7 (trade bdg.) — ISBN-13: 978-0-06-087722-4 (trade bdg.)
ISBN-10: 0-06-087723-5 (pbk.) — ISBN-13: 978-0-06-087723-1 (pbk.)
1. Astronomy—Juvenile literature.  2. Hubble Space Telescope (Spacecraft)—Juvenile literature.
[1. Hubble Space Telescope (Spacecraft)  2. Astronomy.]  I. Title.
QB46 .S543  2002                                                                                          2001024773
520—dc21                                                                                                        CIP
                                                                                                                        AC
1 2 3 4 5 6 7 8 9 10
❖
Revised Edition

## Smithsonian Mission Statement

For more than 160 years, the Smithsonian has remained true to its mission, "the increase and diffusion of knowledge." Today the Smithsonian is not only the world's largest provider of museum experiences supported by authoritative scholarship in science, history, and the arts but also an international leader in scientific research and exploration. The Smithsonian offers the world a picture of America, and America a picture of the world.

## Introduction

How did we get such spectacular photographs of the cosmos? The answer is the Hubble Space Telescope (HST), the most advanced telescope ever built. With the beginning of space shuttle flights in the 1980s, NASA built the telescope so that it could be launched by the shuttle and serviced in space. Ultimately the HST was deployed from the space shuttle in April 1990, and astronomers were excited about its many possible uses. They expected to see through the telescope with much greater resolution than ever before, viewing galaxies as far away as fifteen billion light-years. The results from Hubble touched on some of the most fundamental astronomical questions of humankind, including the existence of black holes and the age of the universe. The telescope has documented in colorful detail the births and deaths of bright celestial objects.

In 2004 NASA announced its decision to end HST's remarkable career. The instrument was aging and becoming difficult to keep operating, but NASA officials are beginning plans to build a new space telescope to replace the Hubble.

*Destination: Space* presents some of the most significant and visually striking images taken by the Hubble Space Telescope. They have altered our view of the cosmos and changed our perspectives on our place in it.

—Roger D. Launius
National Air and Space Museum

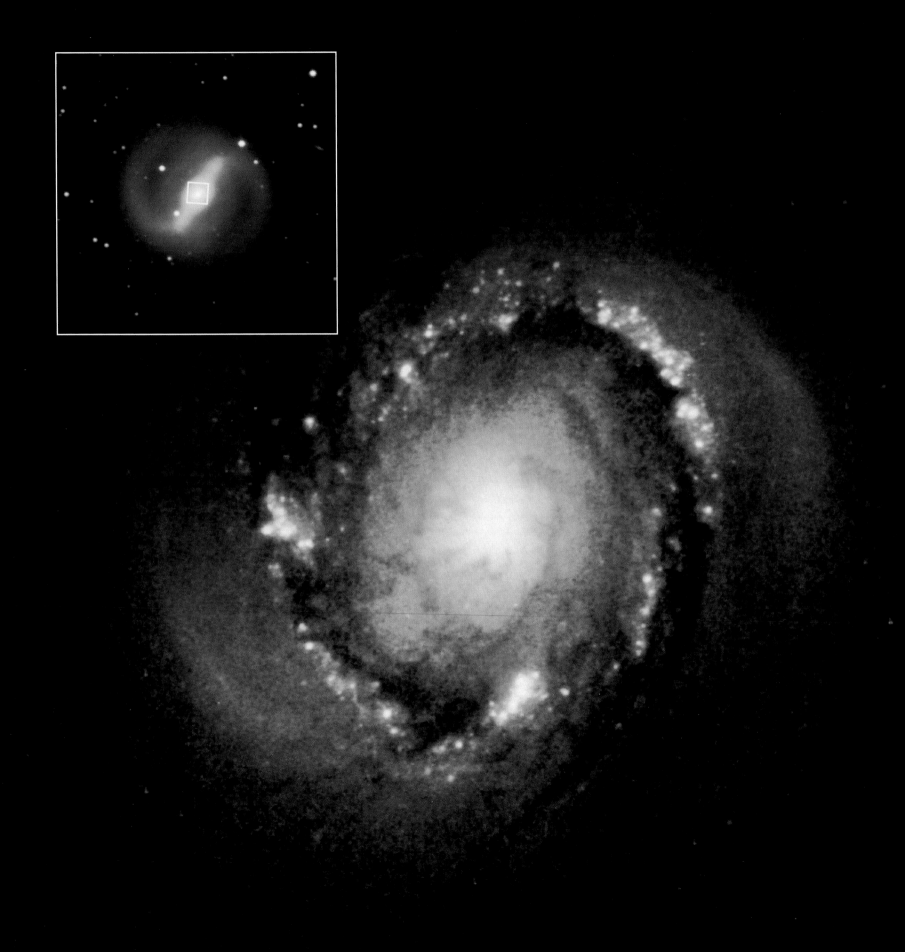

The Hubble Space Telescope, or HST, has been orbiting Earth since April 1990, making 5,800 trips around our planet each year. Above most of the atmosphere, HST is able to see into space ten times more clearly than the best telescopes on Earth. The space telescope takes pictures of objects as near as our Moon and as distant as galaxies at the far edge of the universe.

HST has made many new discoveries, including proof of the existence of black holes. It lets us see where new planets and new stars are born. This photograph shows clusters of newborn stars that formed in a ring around the core of a spiral galaxy in deep space. The infant stars in this galactic nursery were born in a burst of nuclear reactions within the past five million years. Five million years in a medium-sized star's life is equal to a few seconds in a baby's life. Our Sun is a medium-sized star about 4.6 *billion* years old.

HST has taken many photos of planets of our Solar System. These three images of Mars were shot in March 1997, when the red planet was making one of its closest approaches to Earth. Even then Mars was still about sixty million miles away.

The pictures were taken about six hours apart. The timing was chosen so that Mars could be seen from different angles as it rotated during one Martian day. The images show that it is late spring in the planet's northern hemisphere. The north polar cap, which is made up of dry ice (solid carbon dioxide), is rapidly disappearing, showing the much smaller water ice cap beneath.

These images were taken with colored filters. They show a number of bright water ice clouds (apparent right of center on the left image). The colors were chosen to show the difference between airborne dust storms, ice clouds, and Martian surface features.

Saturn is a giant gas planet, the second largest in the Solar System after Jupiter. This is the first picture of the aurora taken by the Space Telescope Imaging Spectrograph (STIS) aboard the HST. The STIS image shows details never before seen of Saturn's spectacular aurora, curtains of light that encircle Saturn's north and south poles and rise more than a thousand miles above the cloud tops.

Saturn's aurora displays are caused by a solar wind that sweeps over the planet. Earth's aurora, sometimes called the Northern or Southern Lights, is similar to Saturn's aurora.

Saturn's rings are the most beautiful of any planet's in our Solar System. The rings are mostly made of chunks of water ice, some as small as your finger, others as big as a house, that whirl around Saturn like swarms of tiny moons. Although it looks as if there are only a few rings, there actually are thousands of smaller ringlets.

This may look like the lights of New York City from an airplane, but it's really part of a star cluster called 47 Tucanae, about fifteen thousand light-years from Earth. One light-year—the distance light can travel in about one year—is equal to about 5.8 trillion miles. A spaceship traveling at ten miles per second would take only five minutes to go from New York to California but more than fifteen years to travel only *one light-year.*

The image taken by HST in July 1999 is a close-up look at a swarm of thirty-five thousand stars near the cluster's central region. The stars are much more tightly packed together here than our Sun and its closest star neighbors. The many yellow stars in the photo are similar to our middle-aged Sun. The red stars are bright red giants near the ends of their lives.

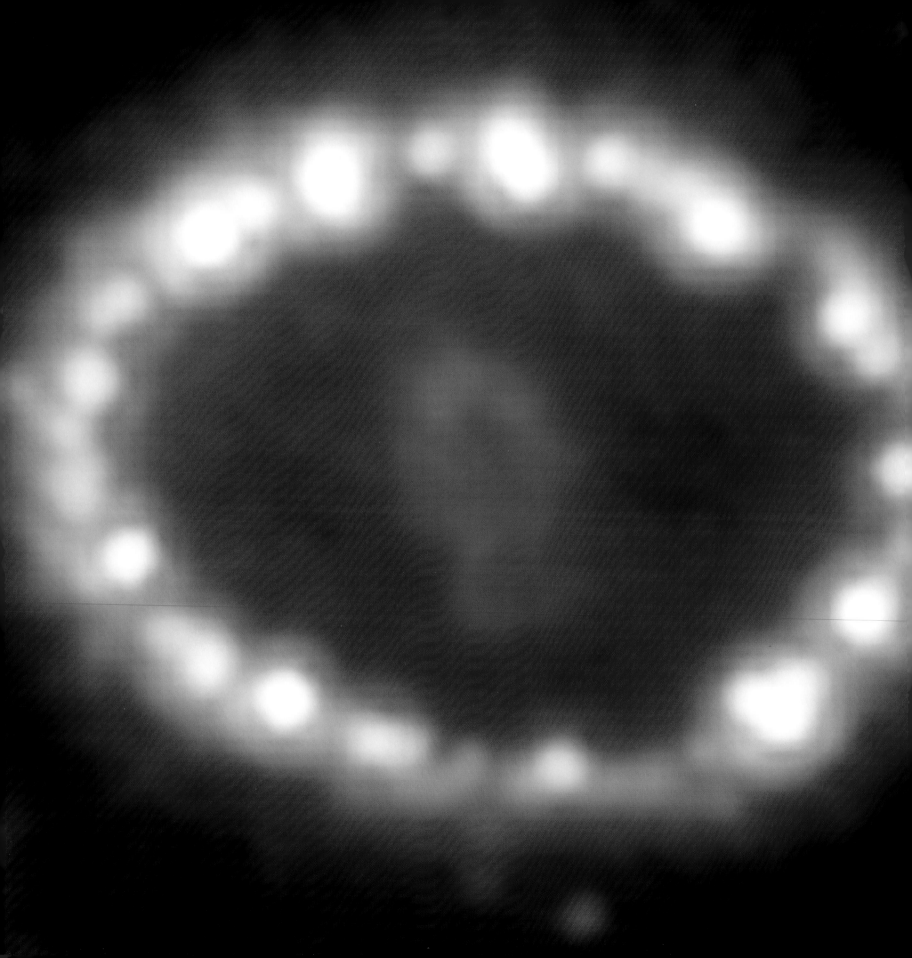

Supernovas are exploding stars that give off enormous amounts of light and energy as they flare brightly and then flicker out and die. For a short time a single supernova can be brighter than an entire galaxy. It can give off as much energy in one day as our Sun does in one million years.

This 2003 HST image shows a ring of glowing gas encircling the site of Supernova 1987A. First discovered on February 23, 1987, the supernova lies in a dwarf galaxy, called the Large Magellanic Cloud, 169,000 light-years away.

Scientists think that the bright ring in the center is caused by radiation from the supernova explosion that lights up the dense gassy material around the dying star. They think that perhaps the two outer rings might be "painted" on the gassy material by a high-energy beam of radiation, like a powerful searchlight sweeping across clouds.

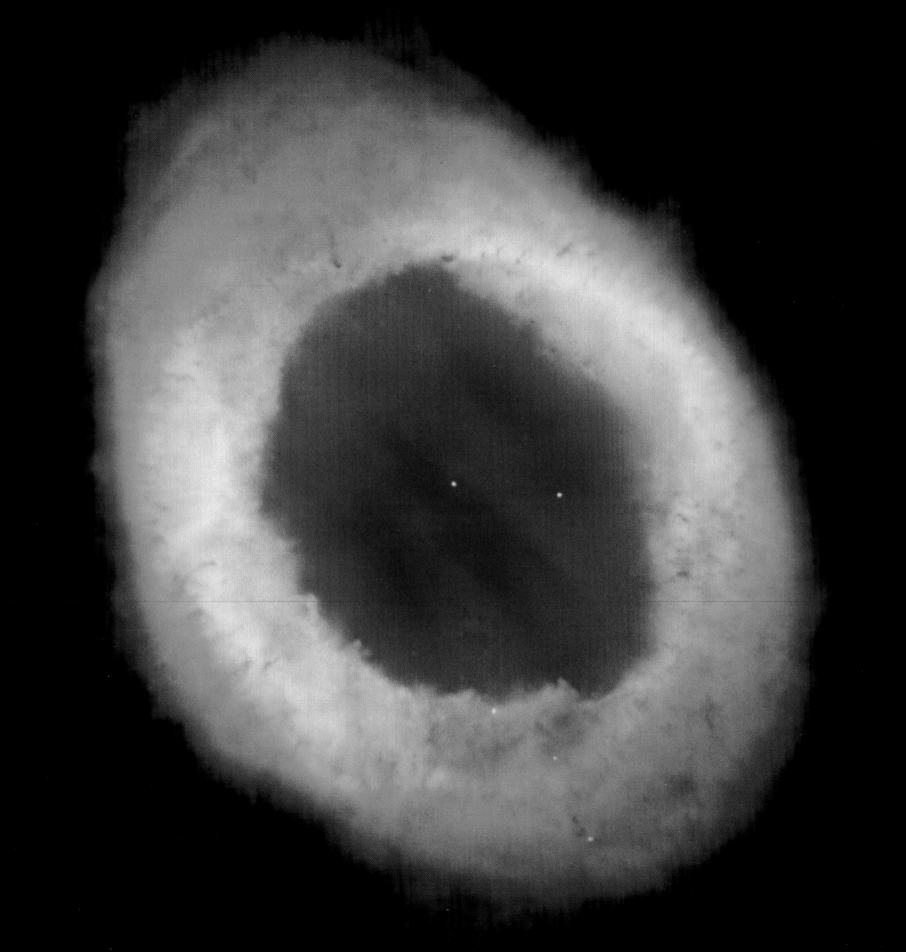

This is an image of huge billowing rings of gas and dust surrounding Eta Carinae, a supergiant star, one of the most massive in the universe, more than one hundred times more massive than our Sun. Eta Carinae radiates about five million times more energy than our Sun. This HST photo is a supersharp view of a doomed star.

For an unknown reason, Eta Carinae suddenly produced a giant outburst of energy about one hundred fifty years ago. It rapidly became one of the brightest stars in the southern sky. The explosion of energy produced a large thin disk surrounded by two giant clouds, all moving outward at about one and a half million miles per hour.

The star remains a puzzle to astronomers, and this image raises even further questions. What caused the star to explode, and why did it explode in such a strange manner? Scientists are studying the clues in this image to find out the answers, not only to this star explosion, but also to others that have been observed.

Stars are born in the dark clouds of hydrogen gas and dust that we call nebulas. This image shows a cluster of newborn stars forming inside the Eagle Nebula, a star-forming region of the Milky Way Galaxy about seven thousand light-years away. The new stars are the bright lights inside the clumps of gas (named EGGS for "evaporating gaseous globules") at the tips of the nebula's trunks, or columns.

A few of these newborn stars are much hotter and as much as one hundred thousand times brighter than our Sun. These young bright stars light up parts of the surrounding nebula, causing the gases to glow like the gas inside a fluorescent lightbulb.

The bright parts of the nebula's columns are rounded blisters on the side of a dense cloud of cold, dark gas in space. Each column of gas is tens of billions of miles across, far larger than the distance from Earth to Pluto.

This HST image of the giant nebula NGC 3603 captures the various stages of the life cycle of stars in a single view. Near the center of this 1999 photo is a star-burst cluster of big, hot, blue, young stars. Waves of radiation and fast stellar winds from these young stars have blown away the gases and left a cavity in the nebula. To the right of the cluster are pillars of gas that are much like the columns of the Eagle Nebula (preceding page). The dark clouds to the top right are probably an earlier stage of star formation.

This single image illustrates the entire life cycle of stars, from dark clouds of gases to young and middle-aged stars to supergiants and their rings that mark the end of the life cycle. From beginning to end, a star's life is measured in billions of years. Our own star, the Sun, is about 4.6 billion years old and is about halfway through its life cycle.

These tadpole-shaped clumps of gases (upper right-hand corner) are exploding from a dying star's final outburst. They are called "cometary knots" because their glowing heads and tails resemble comets. But these mysterious glowing pods are not comets. Each gassy head is at least twice the size of our entire Solar System.

HST has taken pictures of thousands of these knots from a doomed star in the Helix Nebula, a giant cloud of glowing gas and dust about 450 light-years away. Astronomers think that the knots are the result of a collision between hot gases and cooler gases.

No one knows exactly what will happen to the knots. Perhaps they will expand and disappear within a few hundred thousand years. Or perhaps they will clump together and form planets the size of Earth, but frigid and icy. These dark, cold worlds might escape the dying star and roam outward through the universe for billions of years.

This beautiful picture is of a "butterfly" nebula. This cloud of gas and dust around a star called M2–9 is about two thousand light-years away. Another name might be the "Twin Jet Nebula." The central star is one of a very close pair of stars, one of which may be swallowing the other. Scientists think that one of the stars is pulling gases from the surface of the other and flinging them into space, like a pair of exhausts from a super-supersonic jet engine.

The gases in the nebula are traveling at speeds greater than two hundred miles per second, much faster than spaceships. The nebula is enormous; it stretches for ten times the diameter of Pluto's orbit around the Sun.

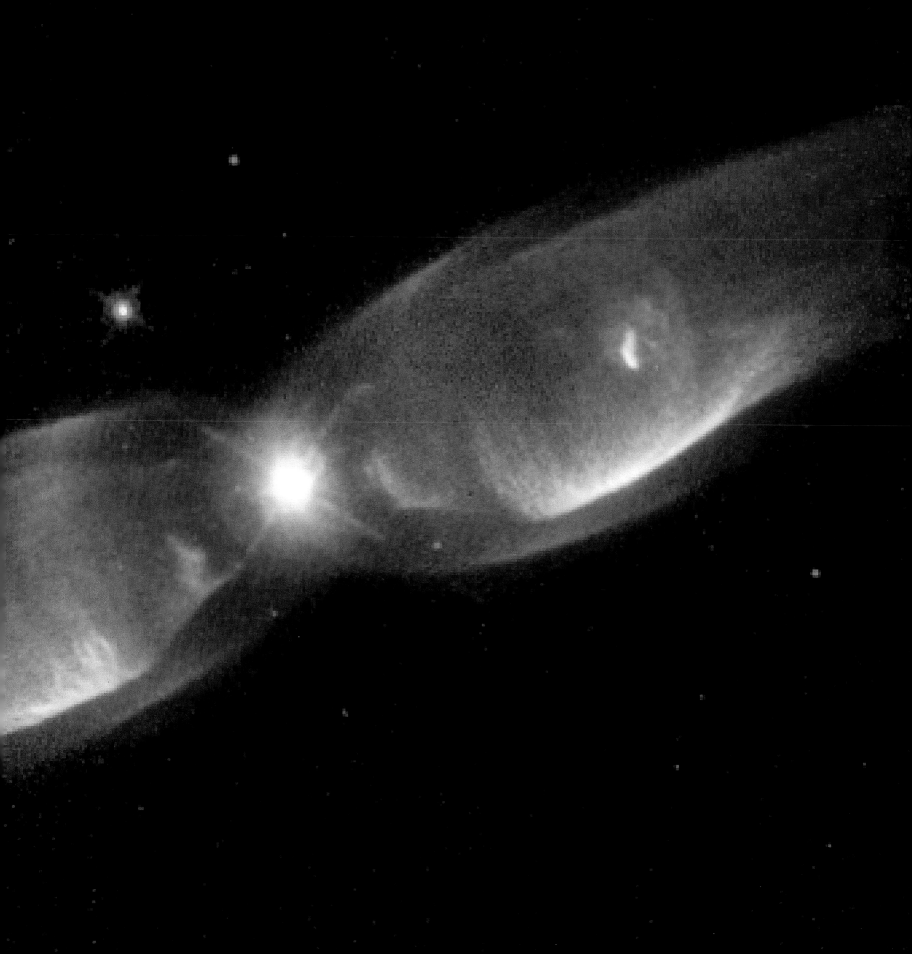

This HST image (the color photograph to the right) pictures a brilliant "fireworks show" at the center of a head-on collision between two galaxies, known as the Antennae Galaxies. In the black-and-white photo at left, over one thousand brilliant blue, young star clusters are shown bursting into life as a result of the wreck. The photo on the left is a ground-based telescopic view of the same event.

In the HST photo the centers of the two galaxies are shown as orange blobs, left and right of the photo's center. The sweeping spiral patterns are traced by bright blue star clusters, the result of a firestorm of star birth triggered by the collision.

The "seeds" for star clusters are huge, dark clouds of cold hydrogen gas. Hot gases heated during the collision squeeze the giant gas clouds, which then collapse under their own gravity. Like a string of firecrackers going off, the clouds of gas light up in a burst of star formation.

What appears to be a bird's head, leaning over to snatch a tasty meal of insects, is another example of two galaxies colliding. A large spiral galaxy takes up the center of the picture, while a smaller passing galaxy is nearly out of view at the lower right. The bright blue "beak" and the blue-white "top feathers" show the path taken by the smaller galaxy.

When galaxies collide, the stars of one galaxy almost never collide with the stars of the other galaxy. That's because the stars are so small compared to the spaces between them.

But the collision is quite different for the two galaxies shown here. When these two galaxies collided, they didn't slide past each other but smashed together because they are mostly made of clouds of gases and tiny particles of matter and dust. Then the gases exploded to form new clusters of stars. The hot blue spots in this image are the areas where stars were born.

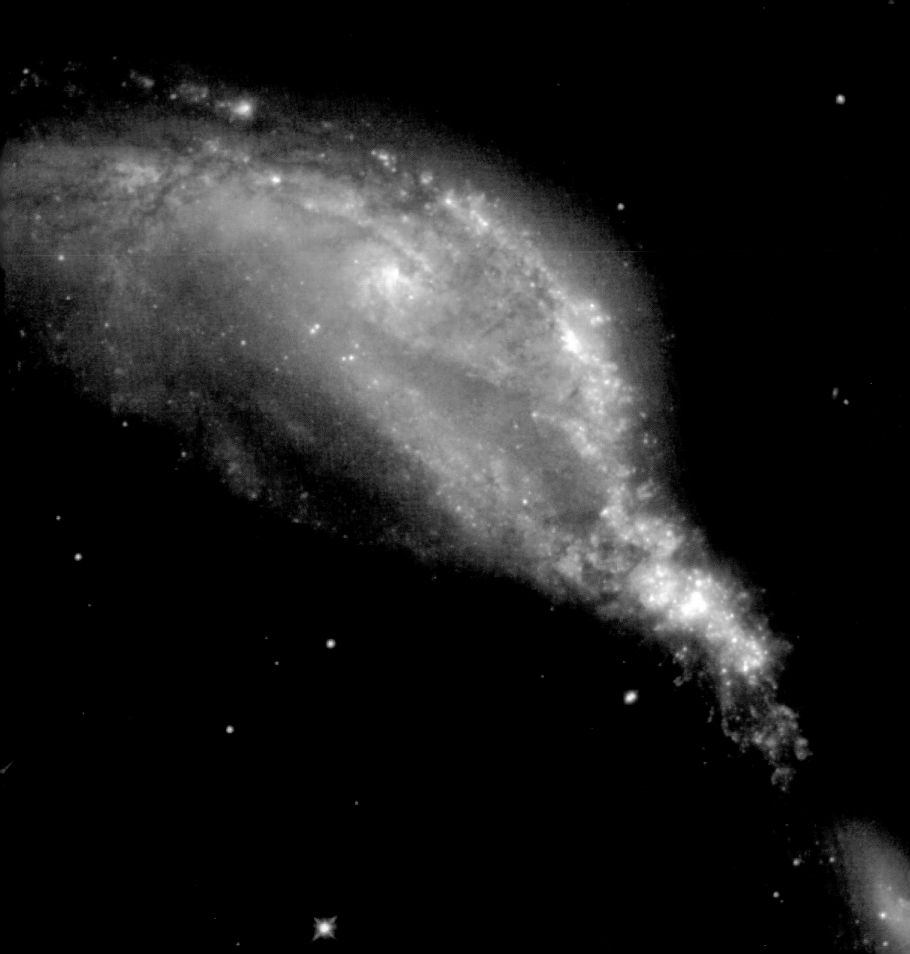

The red crescent in the lower right center of the large picture is an image of a young galaxy that is the farthest ever seen, thirteen billion light-years away. That means that the light from this distant galaxy is only reaching us now after traveling through space for thirteen billion years. The universe is thought to be fourteen billion years old, so we see this galaxy from a time when the universe was very young, only one billion years old.

The galaxy's image is magnified and smeared into an arc shape by the gravitational fields of the galaxies around it that lie much closer to us. These closer galaxies act like a gigantic zoom lens.

The upper left photo is a close-up image of the crescent and shows tiny areas of starbirth activity. The lower left photo is a computer-corrected image that shows details of the crescent five to ten times smaller than HST alone can provide.

Black holes are places where matter is squeezed together so tightly and the pull of gravity is so strong that nothing can escape, not even light.

Black holes come in two sizes: superlarge and small. Superlarge black holes are found at the center of most galaxies, including our own Milky Way. This Hubble Space Telescope image is of an enormous dust disk encircling a superlarge black hole in the center of a distant galaxy. That entire galaxy will be swallowed up by the black hole in several billion years.

Small black holes are usually only a few miles across and are found close to nearby stars. But two black holes were found alone in space by the HST. They were detected because of the way their gravity bent the light of more distant stars behind them. Some scientists think that black holes are common and that many large stars may end their lives as black holes.

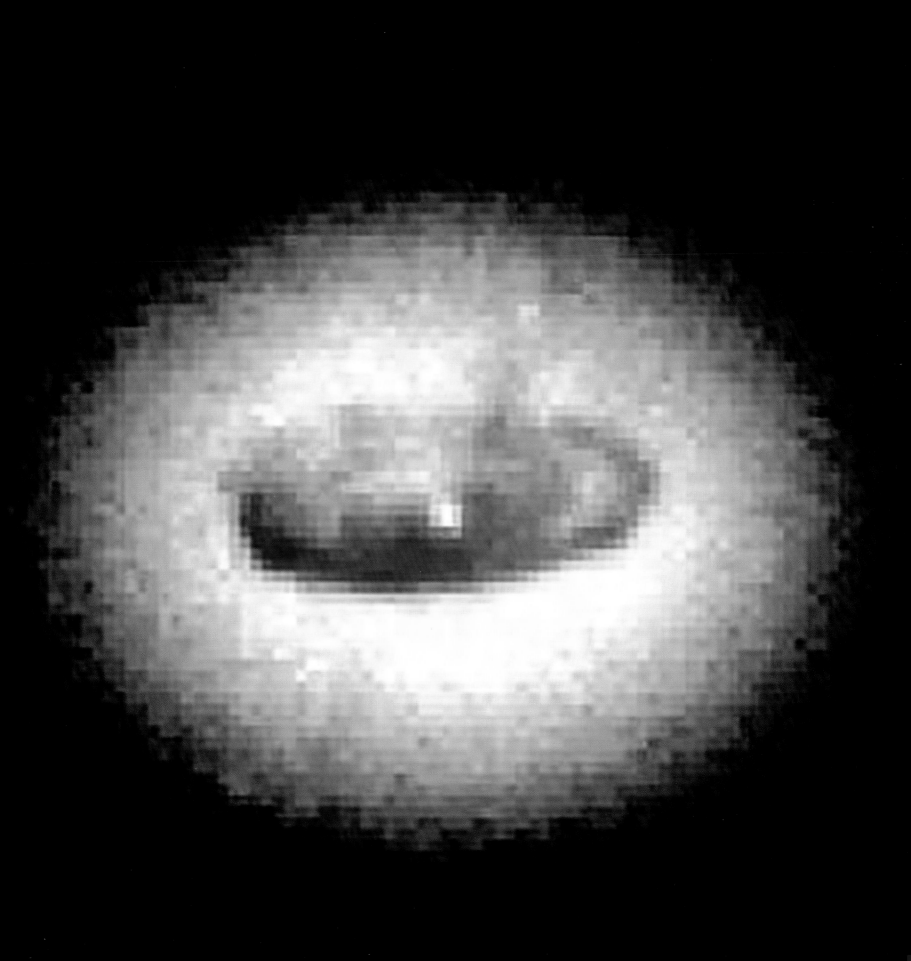

Scientists now think that the universe has more than one hundred billion galaxies and that each galaxy contains about one hundred billion stars. There are more stars in a single galaxy than people now living in every country of the world and ever living throughout history.

Looking at the distant stars and galaxies in this fascinating HST image is both looking into space and looking back with a time machine. The HST shows us events that happened in the earliest ages of the universe. Perhaps the HST will find other planets circling distant stars, including Earth-sized planets. No one knows what new and startling news is still to come from space.